I'd rather Starve than Cook!

A cookbook for people
who hate to cook.

Other books
by
Lisa Orban

MEMOIR SERIES: OKAY, PICTURE THIS...
IT'LL FEEL BETTER WHEN IT QUITS HURTING
WINE COMES IN SIX-PACKS

COOKBOOK
I'D RATHER STARVE THAN COOK!
(a cookbook for people who hate to cook)

VISUAL VIRTEGO:
OPTICAL ILLUSION COLORING BOOKS
VOLUME ONE
VOLUME TWO
VOLUME THREE
VOLUME FOUR

POLITICAL SATIRE
IF I WERE DICTATOR
a tongue-in-cheek guide to saving our democracy

I'd rather Starve than Cook!

Lisa Orban

Indies United Publishing House, LLC
P.O. Box 3071
Quincy, IL 62301-3071

www.indiesunited.net

Second Print Edition September 2018
Published by Indies United Publishing House, LLC

First Print Edition November 2017
First eBook Edition published November 2017

Cover art designed by Lisa M. Orban
Many thanks to Renee for letting me use her kitchen & kids for the cover photo.

ISBN: 978-1-64456-002-0

Indies United Publishing House, LLC
www.indiesunited.net

To my children.

Without your insistence on eating,

I would have starved to death years ago.

HANDY FOOD FINDING GUIDE

*I left you space to add your favorite recipes.

"The most remarkable thing about my mother is that for thirty years she served the family nothing but leftovers. The original meal has never been found."

- Calvin Trillin

I will share a secret with you...

I hate to cook, and there are days that dying of starvation seems like a reasonable plan. And yet, I love cookbooks, I own hundreds of them. I have so many they take up a decent chunk of kitchen storage space. Oh, I don't use them (let's not be silly) but I will occasionally thumb through them, looking at the pictures of food, then discard the idea of making whatever catches my eye when I see the list of ingredients (Gasp! It needs 10 whole items to make?! I feel faint, make it stop!) and firmly shut the book. Nope. Nope. Nope.

Believe me when I tell you, I share your pain at the idea of cooking, every day. Just gives you the shivers, don't it? In an effort to help ease your pain I have put together this cookbook of the many recipes I have created out of sheer laziness and the need to feed my children on a daily basis. Almost everything in this book is grab, open, dump, stir (sometimes), and walk away. There are a few exceptions to this rule, mostly in the Stove Top section, but they also have the advantage of being quick. And most of the recipes only call for a handful of ingredients. There are a few that have a longer list, but for the most part, they require little effort, just open and dump.

So, if you have decided that today cooking is a better option than starving, continue turning pages until something looks worth your efforts. If not, keep this cookbook handy, tomorrow might be your day.

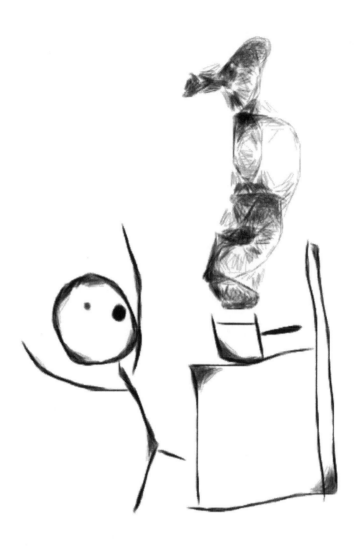

"Part of the secret of success in life is to eat what you like and let the food fight it out inside."

- Mark Twain

 # Crock Pot

The crock pot may be the single most amazing thing ever invented for the lazy cook. I love being able to just grab things from my cabinets and freezer, throw them into the crock pot, and then walk away for hours. (I just have to remember to do all this in the morning, which may be the only downside to it.)

Now, as you go through these recipes, not just in this section but in all of them, you will often see "spice to taste". For me, my fall back spices generally are pepper, garlic, dill, and the mixed spices you can get pretty much everywhere like, Garlic & Herb seasoning, or Hamburger seasoning. Most of the time I have absolutely no idea what I am going to add to any particular meal, it really does depend on my mood more than anything else. So, whenever I am cooking, I will start randomly grabbing spices from my extensive spice rack and sniff them, if it smells good with what I am cooking, I add it, if not, I close it and move on until I'm bored.

I know most cookbook will give you an exact amount of whatever they believe it the perfect amount of whatever spice they want you to use, but the fact is, we all have different tastes, and while a few spices are necessary for various recipes, most are just the personal preference of whoever wrote the cookbook. If it's necessary for the recipe to work, I will add it, if it is not, I'll leave it up to you to decide. If you like your meals spicier, add sriracha, hot sauce or whatever you love that makes you sweat. If you don't like heavily spiced meals, then tone it down to what you are comfortable with.

There will also be options that you can add, or not add. Over the years I have used them, or not, depending on who I am cooking for and allergies. I also add alcohol to some of my recipes, again, they are always optional and by the time whatever is finished cooking is done, it's no longer going to get you drunk. But again, it's entirely up to you.

At the bottom of each page, you will see a note box. Every recipe in this book can be changed or modified to suit your personal tastes, and with that in mind, I've given you space to make your own notes. Go wild, add things, change things, have fun with it. Not a single recipe here is written in stone, so don't be afraid to try something different.

It's your food, be happy with it.

Beef Stew

- ✘ 1 lbs stew meat
- ✘ 1 bag frozen mixed vegetables
- ✘ 2 cans diced stewed tomatoes (optional)
- ✘ a couple of dashes of Worcestershire
- ✘ 1 packet of Lipton soup mix (dry)
- ✘ a few good dashes of Lowery's seasoning salt
- ✘ a few good dashes of any beef related spice that you want, adjust for your tastes
- ✘ a cap full of red cooking wine

Throw everything into crock pot.
Set on low setting.
Stir a few times.
Wait 6 hours.
Done.

Notes:

Philly Cheese Steak

- ✗ 2 lbs stew meat
- ✗ 1 package frozen peppers
- ✗ 1 packet of Lipton onion soup mix
- ✗ 1 cup of water
- ✗ a few dashes of Worcestershire
- ✗ ½ a bottle of steak marinade

*you can also buy a packet of dry steak marinade & add it instead, but if you do add about a 1/2 cup more of water. When I do that, I like using the Peppercorn Steak Marinade, but it will be spicy, you can offset that a bit by adding some honey, but again it will be spicier so only use it if you like a little tingle when you're eating.

Throw into crock pot.
Turn on low.
Stir occasionally.
Wait 6 hours.
Done.

To make sandwiches, you'll also need buns (I prefer the onion Hoagie buns, but even hot dogs buns will do) and a white cheese, sliced, whatever your preference is. I generally use Swiss, but provolone is also good, and for others, I have used pepper jack when they like their sandwich just a touch spicier.

☆☆☆☆☆☆☆☆☆☆☆☆☆☆☆☆☆☆☆☆☆☆☆☆☆☆☆☆☆☆☆☆☆☆☆☆

Notes:

Pot Roast

* ✘ 1 roast (any kind, beef)
* ✘ 1 onion sliced
* ✘ 1 bag frozen carrots
* ✘ 10 potatoes (washed and cubed)
* ✘ 1 packet of Lipton's soup mix
* ✘ a couple of spoons of butter
* ✘ 1 cup of water
* ✘ a dash of cooking sherry (or 4oz of bourbon or whiskey)
* ✘ a dash of Worcestershire sauce
* ✘ spice to taste

Lay roast in the bottom of the crock pot.
Throw everything else into crock pot over it.
Turn on low.
Wait 6 hours.
Done.

Notes:

Roast Beef & Mashed Potatoes

- ✗ 1 roast (any kind, beef)
- ✗ a cup of water
- ✗ 1 packet Lipton soup mix
- ✗ spice to taste
- ✗ 2 jars beef gravy (add to roast when serving)

Throw into crock pot.
Walk away 6 hours.

*Start mashed potatoes 20 minutes before ready to serve.

Mashed Potatoes:

8 – 10 thoroughly cleaned potatoes, diced (you can leave the skins on, I always do since it's the only actual nutritious part of the potato AND I'm lazy)
butter, milk, salt, pepper

In a large pot, add potatoes, fill with water until potatoes are submerged, and a few dashes of salt & a dollop of vegetable oil (it keeps the potatoes from sticking & boiling over)

When it has come to a rolling boil, let cook for about another 10 minutes or until a fork can easily slide into the potatoes.

Drain in colander. Transfer to mixing bowl. Add milk, butter, salt & pepper to taste. Mix well, use a mixer if you have one, hand mash if you don't.

*How much milk & butter you ask? Enough to make it creamy & buttery. So, about a cup or so of milk and about 1 stick of butter.

When done layer: slice of bread – mashed potatoes – roast beef – gravy

☆☆☆☆☆☆☆☆☆☆☆☆☆☆☆☆☆☆☆☆☆☆☆☆☆☆☆☆☆☆☆☆☆☆☆☆☆☆

Notes:

Cube Steak

- ✗ 4 – 8 cube steaks
- ✗ 1 – 2 cans of cream of mushroom soup
- ✗ 1 can mushrooms (don't drain)
- ✗ a few good dashes of pepper
- ✗ a few good dashes of Hamburger spice

Layer bottom with the cube steaks.
Throw everything into crock pot on top.
Set on low setting.
Walk away for 6 hours.

Remove cube steaks mix up gravy.
Done.

☆☆☆☆☆☆☆☆☆☆☆☆☆☆☆☆☆☆☆☆☆☆☆☆☆☆☆☆☆☆☆☆☆☆☆☆☆

Notes:

Chili

- ✗ 1 lb of hamburger (browned)
- ✗ 2 cans of diced stewed tomatoes
- ✗ 2 cans chili beans
- ✗ 1 diced onion
- ✗ 1 teaspoon chili spice
- ✗ a couple of good dashes of pepper
- ✗ 1 beer or 4 oz of either bourbon or whiskey (Optional)
- ✗ 1 bottle of V8 or tomato juice

Throw everything into crock pot.
Set on low setting.
Stir a few times.
Wait 6 hours.
Done.

☆☆☆☆☆☆☆☆☆☆☆☆☆☆☆☆☆☆☆☆☆☆☆☆☆☆☆☆☆☆☆☆☆☆☆☆
Notes:

Crock pot version of Shepard's Pie

- ✗ 1 lb of hamburger (browned)
- ✗ 1 bag of potatoes O'Brian
- ✗ 1 can of green beans (drained)
- ✗ 1 can cream of mushroom soup

Layer in crock pot in this order: hamburger – potatoes O'Brian – green beans – cream of mushroom soup

Turn crock pot on low.
Walk away 6 hours. (Don't stir, at all!)
Done.

☆ ☆

Notes:

<u>Stuffed Green Pepper Soup</u>

- ✗ 1 can of either tomato juice or V8
- ✗ 1 bag frozen diced green peppers
- ✗ 1lb hamburger (browned)
- ✗ 1 can diced stewed tomatoes (I prefer the one with basil, garlic & oregano but you can add them yourself if you don't)
- ✗ 1 cup of instant rice

After browning the hamburger, add all ingredients to crock pot.
Cook for 6 hours on low.
Stir occasionally.
Done.

☆☆☆☆☆☆☆☆☆☆☆☆☆☆☆☆☆☆☆☆☆☆☆☆☆☆☆☆☆☆☆☆☆☆☆☆

Notes:

Maid Rites

- ✘ 1 cup warm water
- ✘ 1 tablespoon dried minced onion
- ✘ 1 beef bouillon cube
- ✘ 1 chicken bouillon cube
- ✘ 2 tablespoons packed light brown sugar
- ✘ 2 tablespoons apple cider vinegar
- ✘ 1 tablespoon soy sauce
- ✘ 2 tablespoons Worcestershire sauce
- ✘ 3 pounds lean ground beef, uncooked

Throw it all in, yes even the uncooked hamburger.
Cook 6 to 10 hours on low.
Stirring occasionally to break up the hamburger.
Done.

Notes:

Easy Swedish Meatballs

- ✘ 1 bag frozen meatballs
- ✘ 2 cans cream of mushroom soup
- ✘ 1 can mushrooms (do not drain)
- ✘ 1 container of sour cream (to be added right before serving
- ✘ spice to taste

Throw everything into crock pot.
Walk away 6 hours. (you might want to stir it on occasion)
Stir in sour cream.
Done.

☆☆☆☆☆☆☆☆☆☆☆☆☆☆☆☆☆☆☆☆☆☆☆☆☆☆☆☆☆☆☆☆☆☆☆☆☆☆

Notes:

BBQed Pulled Pork

- ✗ 1 pork loin
- ✗ either 1 bottle of BBQ sauce (doesn't matter what kind)

OR

- ✗ you can mix 1 jar grape jelly (NOT jam!) & 1 jar shrimp sauce
  (I know, it sounds disgusting but trust me you'll love it)

*If you use BBQ sauce, also add 1 cup of water

Throw into crock pot.
Turn on low.
Wait 6 to 10 hours. (it's done when you can pull the meat apart with a fork)

Pull meat out of crock pot.
Shred meat.

Dump back into crock pot and stir.
Done.

Notes:

Cheese Soup

- ✗ 1 block of Velveeta cheese, cubed
- ✗ 1 container sour cream (add shortly before serving)
- ✗ 1 cup of milk
- ✗ 1 stick of real butter
- ✗ 1 bag stir fry mixed vegetables
- ✗ 1 lb sausage (browned)

Throw in crock pot on low.
Wait 6 hours.
Stir on occasion to keep from burning.
Done.

☆☆☆☆☆☆☆☆☆☆☆☆☆☆☆☆☆☆☆☆☆☆☆☆☆☆☆☆☆☆☆☆☆☆☆☆☆☆

Notes:

"I serve dinner in three phases: serve the food, clear the table, bury the dead."

- Phyllis Diller

 Stove Top

I've never had to bury the dead with my cooking, not even when I first started, but I will admit there were a few meals that probably shouldn't have been allowed to exist in the world with humans. And, there were a few unmitigated disasters that I have never lived down. Like the time I valiantly attempted to make popcorn on the stove. A little oil, a little popcorn, and a little heat. Sounds simple, right?

Well, ten minutes into my attempt, I opened the top of the of the pot, and an amazing amount of thick, black smoke came rolling out instead. Somehow, in that ten-minute time frame, I'd managed to burn the popcorn beyond all recognition and utterly beyond salvage.

It also required me and my roommates to take turns standing outside our apartment door to reassure people that the apartment building was not on fire, only a bit of burnt popcorn until the smoke dissipated. I have to admit that smoke had staying power and ate up about an hour of our lives until it finally left us.

I've never attempted to make popcorn on the stove again.

Chicken Noodle Soup

- ✘ 1 lb boneless chicken breasts
- ✘ 1 package frozen carrots
- ✘ 1 can cream of chicken soup
- ✘ 1 can cream of celery soup
- ✘ 1 package of noodles (I usually use angel hair pasta but you can also use frozen egg noodles, shell pasta or whatever you have on hand. Or you can use rice.)
- ✘ 2 cubes of chicken bullion
- ✘ spice to taste I usually add pepper, garlic, minced onion, and garlic & herb seasoning

In a pot bring chicken, bullion and spices to a boil. Simmer (very low heat) for around an hour with lid on.
Remove chicken when done and shred.

While shredding chicken bring water back to a boil and add pasta or rice.
When pasta is done add all other ingredients, stir and let simmer for about 10 minutes.
Done.

☆ ☆

Notes:

Hungarian Goulash

- ✗ 1 lb stew meat
- ✗ 2 cans of diced tomatoes
- ✗ 1 packet of Lipton's soup mix
- ✗ a dash of Worcestershire sauce
- ✗ a dash of pepper, garlic and minced onion
- ✗ butter

Melt butter on medium heat in a big skillet.
Brown stew meat on medium heat.
Add all other ingredients and simmer for about 15 minutes.
Serve over mashed potatoes.
Done.

Mashed Potatoes:

8 – 10 thoroughly cleaned potatoes, diced (you can leave the skins on, I always do since it's the only actual nutritious part of the potato AND I'm lazy)
butter, milk, salt, pepper

In a large pot, add potatoes, fill with water until potatoes are submerged, and a few dashes of salt & a dollop of vegetable oil (it keeps the potatoes from sticking & boiling over)

When it has come to a rolling boil, let cook for about another 10 minutes or until a fork can easily slide into the potatoes.

Drain in colander. Transfer to mixing bowl. Add milk, butter, salt & pepper to taste. Mix well, use a mixer if you have one, hand mash if you don't.

(How much milk & butter you ask? Enough to make it creamy & buttery. So, about a cup or so of milk and about 1 stick of butter.)

☆☆
Notes:

__Goulash__

- ✗ 1 lb of hamburger (browned)
- ✗ 1 diced onion (optional)
- ✗ 1 can of diced tomatoes
- ✗ 1 can of tomato soup
- ✗ 1 package of frozen corn
- ✗ 1 package of elbow macaroni
- ✗ 1 packet Lipton's soup mix
- ✗ a dash of cooking sherry
- ✗ spice to taste

In a skillet brown hamburger with diced onion.
Drain grease and set aside.

In a big pot, add macaroni to boiling water. Follow the directions on the box.
When done, drain and return to pot.

Add all other ingredients. Stir occasionally while simmering on medium/low heat around 10
to 15 minutes.
You can also add cheese of any variety to this.
Done.

Notes:

Hamburger with Mushroom Gravy

- ✗ 1 – 2 lbs of hamburger (browned)
- ✗ 1 – 2 cans of cream of mushroom soup
- ✗ 1 packet of Lipton's soup mix
- ✗ 1 jar of mushrooms (optional)
- ✗ pepper

In a skillet brown hamburger.
Drain grease and return to skillet.
In the skillet add everything together, stir until warm and serve over bread.
Done.

☆☆☆☆☆☆☆☆☆☆☆☆☆☆☆☆☆☆☆☆☆☆☆☆☆☆☆☆☆☆☆☆☆☆☆☆☆☆☆

Notes:

<u>Sloppy Joe's</u>

- ✗ 1 – 2 lbs of hamburger (browned)
- ✗ ketchup, mustard, BBQ sauce (any kind)
- ✗ 1 finely diced onion

In a skillet brown hamburger with diced onion.
Drain grease and return to skillet.

Add an equal amount of ketchup, mustard and BBQ sauce.
Stir until warm.

Serve on buns, garnish with whatever makes you happy.
Done.

☆☆☆☆☆☆☆☆☆☆☆☆☆☆☆☆☆☆☆☆☆☆☆☆☆☆☆☆☆☆☆☆☆☆

Notes:

Spaghetti & Meatballs

✗   1 - box of angel hair pasta (or you can use spaghetti noodles, but I think they're too thick)

✗   1 - 2 cans of spaghetti sauce (any kind will do)

✗   1 bag of frozen meatballs

✗   1 can of diced tomatoes (I prefer using the one with garlic, onion and oregano)

✗   pepper, garlic, dill, steak seasoning

*If you're wanting to sneak in some vegetables into your kids without them noticing, get a bag of frozen mixed veggies and run through a food processor and add it to the spaghetti sauce. They'll never notice. Trust me.

Make pasta according to directions. Drain.

Put meatballs in the oven to warm according to directions.

In another pot, add spaghetti sauce, tomatoes, (minced veggie if you decide to add them) and spices heat on medium, stirring frequently.

When everything is done, pour everything into sauce pot, stir thoroughly. Warm on medium heat for about 10 minutes.
Done.

*If you'd like, you can sprinkle with shredded cheese before you serve the spaghetti.

☆ ☆

Notes:

Taco Macaroni

- ✗ 1 lb of hamburger (browned)
- ✗ 1 packet of taco mix
- ✗ 2 boxes of macaroni & cheese
- ✗ milk & butter

In a skillet brown hamburger.
Drain grease and set aside.

In a pot make macaroni & cheese according to directions.

When the mac & cheese is done add taco mix, and hamburger.
Warm on medium low heat for about 10 minutes.

You can also add diced tomatoes, onions or additional cheese if you'd like.
Done.

*If you'd like it creamier, instead of milk use sour cream.

☆☆

Notes:

Hobo Stew

- ✗ 1 lb hamburger or 1 package cut up hot dogs.
- ✗ 2 can of chili beans
- ✗ ¼ of a cup of brown sugar
- ✗ ketchup (use can substitute with a can of tomato soup)

After browning and draining hamburger, add chili beans & brown sugar and then add enough ketchup to coat everything.

OR

if you are using hot dogs, add everything at once.

Cook on medium low heat for about 10 minutes.
Done.

☆☆☆☆☆☆☆☆☆☆☆☆☆☆☆☆☆☆☆☆☆☆☆☆☆☆☆☆☆☆☆☆☆☆☆☆

Notes:

Jambalaya

- ✘ 1 package of Kielbasa (you can use Little Smokies if you prefer)
- ✘ 1 lb of shrimp (optional)
- ✘ 1 package of mixed frozen peppers
- ✘ 2 cans of diced tomatoes
- ✘ 1 package of frozen corn
- ✘ 2 cups of instant rice
- ✘ 2 cups of water
- ✘ some butter
- ✘ a dash of Cajan spice
- ✘ a dash of red cooking wine
- ✘ a dash of garlic & add spices to taste

In a big skillet add butter, melt on medium heat.
When melted add cut up Kielbasa & shrimp.

Cook on medium for about 10 minutes. If you added shrimp when they pink up, it's ready.

Add everything but the rice & water, cook an additional 10 minutes.
Then add rice & water, cover with lid, and simmer until rice is done.

And, you're done!

☆☆☆☆☆☆☆☆☆☆☆☆☆☆☆☆☆☆☆☆☆☆☆☆☆☆☆☆☆☆☆☆☆☆☆☆☆☆

Notes:

Easy Stir-Fry

- ✘ 1 package of frozen vegetable mix
- ✘ 1 lb chicken, shrimp or stew meat
- ✘ 2 cups of rice
- ✘ 2 cups of water
- ✘ 1 egg
- ✘ soy sauce
- ✘ olive oil
- ✘ Sake (not necessary, but it does give the food a nice flavor)

In a pot boil 2 cups of water. Once it has been brought to a boil, add rice, stir and cover. Remove from heat and let sit for at least 10 minutes or until all the water is absorbed.

While the rice is doing its thing, heat up your wok (a frying pan works if you don't own a wok) on med-high heat.
It is ready when you sprinkle a few drops of water on it and it hisses.
Cover bottom with a thin layer of olive oil let heat up for about a minute then add your meat. Thoroughly cook.

Then add your bag of frozen vegetables.
When the vegetables are cooked, but still crisp, add soy sauce. Keep stirring for about 5 minutes. When done, transfer to a serving bowl.

While your wok (frying pan) is still hot, add a bit of soy sauce then add egg. Scramble.
Add the Sake and rice, add a bit more soy sauce, and stir until mixed.
Remove from heat, and serve with stir-fry.
Done.

   *If you rather not use soy sauce, you can substitute garlic sauce.

☆☆☆☆☆☆☆☆☆☆☆☆☆☆☆☆☆☆☆☆☆☆☆☆☆☆☆☆☆☆☆☆☆☆☆☆

Notes:

Biscuits & Gravy

- ✗ 1 lb of country sausage
- ✗ milk
- ✗ flour
- ✗ salt, pepper, dill & garlic
- ✗ biscuits (follow directions on the can)

Brown sausage, breaking it up into small pieces.
When done, DO NOT drain grease.

Lower heat and add milk, flour & spices.
The ratio is about ¼ of a cup of flour for every 2 cups of milk.

Using a whisk, continually stir until desired consistency is reached.
Immediately remove from heat and serve over biscuits.
Done.

☆☆☆☆☆☆☆☆☆☆☆☆☆☆☆☆☆☆☆☆☆☆☆☆☆☆☆☆☆☆☆☆☆☆☆☆☆

Notes:

Sh*t on a Shingle

- ✗ 2 packages of beef Budding lunch meat
- ✗ butter
- ✗ milk
- ✗ flour
- ✗ salt, pepper, dill & garlic
- ✗ toast

Cut up lunch meat into strips.
In a skillet turn on medium heat, melt butter.

When the butter is melted, add beef.
Stir around for about 2 – 4 minutes, until edges curl.

Lower heat and add milk, flour & spices.
The ratio is about ¼ of a cup of flour for every 2 cups of milk.

Using a whisk, continually stir until desired consistency is reached.
Immediately remove from heat and serve over toast.
Done.

☆☆☆☆☆☆☆☆☆☆☆☆☆☆☆☆☆☆☆☆☆☆☆☆☆☆☆☆☆☆☆☆☆☆☆☆

Notes:

"Fettuccine Alfredo is macaroni and cheese for adults."

- Mitch Hedberg

 Oven

The kitchen and I have never been good friends, and I sometimes secretly believe it may be out to get me for all the problems I have encountered in it. If I could avoid ever going in there, except to get ice for my drink, I probably would. In my life, I've had more cuts, bumps, and bruises from appliances, three fires, an exploding stove, and once even an exploded salmon.

No, really, an exploding fish.

I was making a Father's Day dinner for my dad right after he had found out he had high cholesterol and would no longer be able to enjoy many of the foods he loved. Wanting to make him feel better, I did something I don't normally do, I put effort into a meal. The menu consisted of baked salmon, wild rice pilaf, spinach stuffed mushrooms, green beans with diced tomatoes, and an angel food cake covered in fresh strawberries.

And everything was going great. I prepped all the food, had this and that cooking on the stove top, the mushrooms in the oven, and set the salmon aside to pop in the oven last, on an unused burner in the back. (I have a very small kitchen with very little counter space, so the back burner was the only place available that wasn't currently in use.)

Turning my back on the meal to put a dish in the dishwasher I heard a loud POP! and felt something strike me in the back. Giving a little scream, I jumped as I turned, to see the Pyrex baking dish had developed a large crack with several missing pieces. In my haste, I'd stupidly turned on the wrong burner and exploded the dish, salmon and all.

I learned that day that while a Pyrex dish does just fine with oven heat, putting it on a heated burner is a very, very bad idea!

I did manage to salvage the meal, and we did have salmon, and my dad absolutely loved it.

But, for about two seconds I thought I had been shot in the back, and it scared me to death. My life flashed before my eyes faster than the salmon could finish its trip to my ceiling. To this day, I always, always, double checked which burner I have on before I sit anything on my stove.

Baked Salmon

- ✘ salmon (this also works with any kind of white fish)
- ✘ 1 cup mayo
- ✘ 1 cup Parmesan cheese
- ✘ a dash of salt, pepper and dill
- ✘ cooking spray

In a baking dish, cover in cooking spray. Add salmon, skin side down.
In a small mixing bowl, add mayo, Parmesan cheese and spices. Mix well.

Cover salmon with mixture.

Bake uncovered in oven at 450 for about 12 - 15 minutes.
Done.

*If you'd like, you can add a bit of diced tomato or baby spinach over the mayo mixture.

Notes:

Italian Chicken

- ✗ 1 cut up fryer
- ✗ 1 bottle of Italian dressing
- ✗ cooking spray

✗

Coat a baking dish with cooking spray.
Add chicken.
Coat with Italian dressing.

Bake at 450 for about an hour.
Yes, seriously. Two ingredients. It doesn't get any easier than that!
Done.

☆☆☆☆☆☆☆☆☆☆☆☆☆☆☆☆☆☆☆☆☆☆☆☆☆☆☆☆☆☆☆☆☆☆☆☆☆

Notes:

Chicken Pot Pie

- ✗ 2 – 3 uncooked boneless chicken breasts, cubed
- ✗ 1 package mixed vegetables
- ✗ 1 can cream of chicken soup
- ✗ 1 jar of chicken gravy
- ✗ biscuit mix & water
- ✗ spice to taste
- ✗ cooking spray

In a sprayed baking dish, add uncooked chicken, vegetables, soup and gravy, add spices, mix well.

In a separate bowl, mix up biscuit mix, but make it thinner than the directions call for, you want to be able to pour it over the top evenly.
Think cake batter consistency.

Add any spices you'd like to the biscuit mix.
Pour over the top. Smooth.
Bake in oven at 350 until the biscuits on top are done.

Usually around 30 to 45 minutes depending on how thick you made them. You can check by sliding a knife into the biscuits, when it comes out clean, it's done.

☆☆☆☆☆☆☆☆☆☆☆☆☆☆☆☆☆☆☆☆☆☆☆☆☆☆☆☆☆☆☆☆☆☆☆☆☆☆
Notes:

Chicken & Rice

- ✗ 1 cut up fryer
- ✗ 1 can of cream of mushroom soup
- ✗ 2 cans of cream of chicken soup
- ✗ paprika
- ✗ instant rice
- ✗ water
- ✗ cooking spray

In a sprayed baking dish, cover the bottom with rice.
Add 1 can of cream of mushroom soup and 1 can of cream of chicken soup.
Mix, using water to thin out enough to thoroughly cover all the rice.

Add whatever spices make you happy.

Then place chicken on top of rice.
Use remaining can of cream of chicken to cover the chicken.
Sprinkle with paprika.

Bake at 450 for about an hour.
Done.

☆☆

Notes:

Chicken Cacciatore

- ✗   1 cut up fryer
- ✗   1 can of diced tomatoes
- ✗   1 package of Lipton's soup mix
- ✗   1 diced onion
- ✗   1 jar of spaghetti sauce
- ✗   1 box of spaghetti noodles (cooked according to the directions)
- ✗   cooking spray

In a sprayed baking dish, place uncooked chicken at the bottom.
In a bowl mix all other ingredients expect noodles, and pour over chicken.

Bake in oven at 450 for about an hour to an hour and a half.

When chicken is done, stir remain sauce thoroughly.
On plate, put cooked spaghetti, add chicken then a ladle sauce over the top.
Done.

   *You can also take a bag of mixed stir fry vegetables, run through food processor and add to baking dish with the rest of the ingredients if you'd like to get a few more veggies into your kids without a fuss.

☆☆☆☆☆☆☆☆☆☆☆☆☆☆☆☆☆☆☆☆☆☆☆☆☆☆☆☆☆☆☆☆☆☆☆☆☆☆
Notes:

Parmesan Chicken Lasagna

- ✗ 3 chicken breasts cooked and shredded
- ✗ 1 large container of cottage cheese
- ✗ 1 bag of white shredded cheese
- ✗ 1 cup of Parmesan
- ✗ 1 jar of Alfredo sauce
- ✗ spices: dill, garlic, onion, oregano
- ✗ 1 box of uncooked lasagna noodles
- ✗ cooking spray

In a bowl mix chicken, Parmesan, cottage cheese, Alfredo sauce and spices.

In a sprayed cooking dish layer as follows:
uncooked noodles, chicken mixture, cheese.
Continue to layer until the top is reached, cheese being the last layer.

Bake at 375 for about an hour.

Checking often to make sure the top is not burning. If it is, but the noodles aren't done, lower temp to 350 and continue cooking until noodle are soft.
Done.

   *You can also add mushrooms, onion or shredded spinach to this dish. Add it to the chicken mix if you do.

☆ ☆
Notes:

Chicken Alfredo

- ✘ 3 chicken breasts - cut & cubed
- ✘ 1 jar of Alfredo sauce
- ✘ 1 jar of mushrooms
- ✘ 1 container of sour cream
- ✘ ½ a cup of Parmesan cheese
- ✘ spices: I usually add garlic, onion, dill, oregano
- ✘ 1 container of baby spinach shredded (optional)
- ✘ cooking spray

In a sprayed baking dish add all the ingredients, stir well.
Add a handful of shredded cheese on top and sprinkle with oregano & dill.

Bake at 350 for about 45 minutes
(but check at 30 because sometimes it gets done faster and you don't want it to burn)
Done.

*You can serve this with almost any kind of noodle you have handy or none at all. Your choice.

*If you want to bake it in with the chicken, shorter noodles like rotini works best. But you'll need to cook the noodles before mixing in.

*If you are going to mix it afterwords, fettuccine or egg noodles would be my recommendation.

☆☆☆☆☆☆☆☆☆☆☆☆☆☆☆☆☆☆☆☆☆☆☆☆☆☆☆☆☆☆☆☆☆☆

Notes:

Apple Honey Glazed Chicken

- ✗ 1 whole chicken
- ✗ 1 apple (I prefer red delicious, cut into quarters)
- ✗ honey
- ✗ plain BBQ sauce
- ✗ cooking spray

Coat baking dish with cooking spray.
Add chicken (remove any giblets they may have put inside whole chicken) and stuff with apple.

In a small mixing bowl, pour equal amounts honey and BBQ sauce, mix.
(You can also add any spices you'd like. I generally use a grill seasoning mix)

Coat top of chicken with honey mixture.

Bake at 350 for about an hour and half. Depending on how big your chicken is it might take a bit longer or shorter time to cook.
Done.

   *It's done with the legs fall to the sides and there's no pink to be seen.

☆☆☆☆☆☆☆☆☆☆☆☆☆☆☆☆☆☆☆☆☆☆☆☆☆☆☆☆☆☆☆☆☆☆☆

Notes:

Tune Casserole

- ✘ 1 can of undrained tuna (in water)
- ✘ 1 package of frozen peas (can also use peas & carrot mix)
- ✘ 1 can of cream of mushroom soup
- ✘ 1 box of elbow macaroni (cooked according to directions)
- ✘ 1 container of french onions (or can use crumbled saltine crackers)
- ✘ cooking spray (I prefer the butter kind, but anything to keep it from sticking to the pan will work)

In a sprayed baking dish, add all ingredients, except the french onions, mix well.
Smooth mixture so it's level.

Add french onions or crackers on top.

Bake at 350 for a half hour.
Done.

☆ ☆

Notes:

Cheesy Tuna Casserole

- ✗ 1 can of tuna (can also substitute cooked shredded chicken)
- ✗ 2 boxes of macaroni & cheese (cook according to directions)
- ✗ milk & butter
- ✗ 1 can of cream of chicken soup
- ✗ 1 diced onion
- ✗ cheese slices
- ✗ cooking spray

In a sprayed baking dish, add all ingredients, mix well. Smooth top, and add enough cheese slices to cover the top.

Bake at 350 for a half hour.
Done.

☆☆

Notes:

Shepherd's Pie

- ✗ 1 lb hamburger (browned & drained)
- ✗ 1 package of frozen corn
- ✗ mashed potatoes (approx. 10 potatoes worth)
- ✗ 1 package of shredded cheese (almost any kind will do)
- ✗ 2 cans of cream of mushroom soup
- ✗ cooking spray

In a sprayed baking dish, layer ingredients as follows:
hamburger mixed with cream of mushroom soup – corn – half your shredded cheese – mashed potatoes – remaining shredded cheese

Bake at 375 for about a ½ hour or until cheese is melted and the edges have a light golden brown color.
Done.

   *You can also substitute tater tots for the mashed potatoes, but if you do that, increase heat to 425 for about 30 minutes and put all your cheese in the middle layer.

☆ ☆
Notes:

Meatloaf

Okay, for this we're going to get creative. This is the list of basic ingredients you should have, but to be truthful, all you really have to have is the hamburger, everything else can be substituted with something else.

- ✗ 2 – 3 lbs of hamburger (you can also use a hamburger/sausage mix)
- ✗ 1 egg
- ✗ 1 package of stuffing (any kind you like)
- ✗ whatever spices make you happy
- ✗ cooking spray

Now, things get creative from here. You can use any of the following ingredients, just make sure you have enough liquid ingredients to coat all of the hamburger evenly. And feel free to mix and match. The one I use the most is ketchup/mustard/BBQ sauce but have fun with it. Just keep in mind, you should have some kind of tomato base to it for it to taste like meatloaf.

ketchup – mustard – BBQ sauce (any kind) – horseradish – Worcestershire – A1 – a can of tomato soup (as a substitute for ketchup) - a can of cheese soup (if you do this, use less ketchup/mustard) - steak sauce of any kind

Other fillers:
mushrooms - bacon bits - shredded cheese (any kind) - diced tomatoes - onions - peppers (any kind) - Lipton dry soup mix (I prefer garlic & herb)

Go crazy, experiment, have fun. I make it different every time and nobody complains.

   *If you don't have stuffing, you can also substitute a cup of uncooked rice, crushed crackers (pretty much any kind), 8 slices of stale bread (any kind), 2 cups of plain oatmeal or a small box of wild rice. I've never used croutons, but in theory they should work as well.
   *If you don't have an egg, you can use 2 tablespoons of olive oil.

After you've collected your ingredients, mix them all together in a bowl. When thoroughly mixed, transfer to a sprayed baking dish. Form into a half football, about an inch away from the sides. Add a glaze of ketchup or mustard or BBQ sauce or even all three, smooth over top. (You can also add bacon strips after the glaze if you're so inclined)

Bake in oven for about an hour at 425. Remove from oven, let sit for about 10 minutes then drain the grease. Done.

☆ ☆

Notes:

Tin Foil Meal

- ✗ 1 lb of uncooked hamburger
- ✗ 1 package of frozen corn
- ✗ 1 package potatoes O'brian
- ✗ butter
- ✗ tin foil
- ✗ whatever spices make you happy

Make four tin foil square about 8 inches on each side. Set aside.

Divide the hamburger into 4 equal portions.
    *If you're going to add any spices, do it before you divide up the hamburger.
Roll hamburger into a ball.

Place in the center of the tinfoil.
Add corn and potatoes O'Brian around the hamburger and a dollop of butter.

Fold tinfoil over the mix securely.
Throw in oven at 350 for about 30 to 45 minutes depending on the size of the hamburger balls you've made.
Open tin foil, done.

    *You can also make this on the grill, over a campfire, in the crock pot, or in a roaster oven.

☆☆☆☆☆☆☆☆☆☆☆☆☆☆☆☆☆☆☆☆☆☆☆☆☆☆☆☆☆☆☆☆☆☆☆☆☆☆☆
Notes:

Swiss Steak

- ✘ 1 round steak
- ✘ 1 sliced onion
- ✘ 1 – 2 cans of stewed tomatoes
- ✘ 1 packet of Lipton's soup mix
- ✘ 1 cube beef bullion (dissolved in 1 cup of water)
- ✘ cooking spray

Place round steak in sprayed baking dish.
Cover with onion.

Mix soup mix with bullion and stewed tomatoes, then pour over steak.

Bake in oven at 375 until it's gotten to the level of pink you want in a steak.
So about 15 to 45 minutes depending on your preferences.
Done.

☆☆☆☆☆☆☆☆☆☆☆☆☆☆☆☆☆☆☆☆☆☆☆☆☆☆☆☆☆☆☆☆☆☆☆☆☆☆☆

Notes:

Rubin Casserole

- 4 packages of Budding either corned beef, beef or pastrami
- 1 onion sliced
- 3 eggs
- ½ a cup of Thousand Island dressing
- ½ a loaf of cubed marble & rye bread
- 1 package of Swiss cheese
- cooking spray

In a sprayed baking dish layer as follows:
meat – onion - 1/3 cheese – 1/3 bread
Continue to layer until you reach the top with bread being the last layer

Mix egg & dressing together & pour over the top evenly

Bake at 350 for about a ½ hour.
Done.

☆☆☆☆☆☆☆☆☆☆☆☆☆☆☆☆☆☆☆☆☆☆☆☆☆☆☆☆☆☆☆☆☆☆☆☆
Notes:

Kielbasa Casserole

- ✖ 1 package of Kielbasa (you can substitute Little Smokies)
- ✖ 1 bag of frozen corn
- ✖ 1 bag of potatoes O'Brian
- ✖ 1 stick of melted butter
- ✖ cooking spray

*You can add 6 whipped eggs if you want to make it more of a breakfast casserole.

Dice up Kielbasa into bite sized pieces and layer in sprayed cooking dish.
Add corn and potatoes O'Brian.

Pour melted butter over the top.
   *If you decide to use eggs, use only a half a stick of butter instead.

Bake at 425 for half an hour.
Done.

☆☆☆☆☆☆☆☆☆☆☆☆☆☆☆☆☆☆☆☆☆☆☆☆☆☆☆☆☆☆☆☆☆☆☆☆

Notes:

Breakfast Bake

- ✗ a dozen eggs
- ✗ potatoes O'Brian
- ✗ can of mushrooms
- ✗ 1- diced onion
- ✗ 1lb - sausage (browned)
- ✗ 1 cup of water
- ✗ 1 bag shredded cheese (any kind)
- ✗ salt - pepper - dill - garlic
- ✗ cooking spray

In a baking dish, use the cooking spray to coat the bottoms and the sides.

In a bowl, crack a dozen eggs, add water and mix until thoroughly combined.

In baking dish, put down the potatoes O'Brian, then layer with sausage, cheese, onions and mushrooms.
Pour egg mixture over it all.

Cover in tinfoil and bake at 425 for around 45 minutes. Start checking the center at around 30 minutes. If your knife comes out (mostly) clean, it is done.
(because of the cheese, your knife with always have some gooey remains on it, even if it's completely done)

☆☆☆☆☆☆☆☆☆☆☆☆☆☆☆☆☆☆☆☆☆☆☆☆☆☆☆☆☆☆☆☆☆☆☆☆☆☆

Notes:

"When a man's stomach is full it makes no difference whether he is rich or poor."

- Euripides

Cheap & Easy

There have been times in my life when I have had next to nothing to eat, and a baloney sandwich, with cheese, was considered a luxury. As a matter of fact, there was once a time in my life that I lived off of nothing but Hostess snack cakes and water for a week. I still can't look at a Zinger in the eye without feeling a bit queasy.

When I was 18-years-old I jumped into a Toyota truck with two kittens and one of my closest friends from high school and drove off into the sunset, to make our home in Phoenix, AZ. Nothing from the first turn out of the driveway to our arrival worked out as we'd planned, including the apartment we were supposed to move into falling through.

Quickly going through my savings finding a new apartment, turning on utilities and all the other additional unexpected costs I didn't think we'd have to come up with, left us with an apartment to live in, but bare cupboards.

Sending my friend out with the last of our money to purchase food, I stayed behind to finish settling us in. She'd been living in Phoenix for two years prior to my arrival and knew her way around and she seemed the logical choice to send out to do the shopping.

I was wrong.

Two hours later she walked back into our apartment proudly carrying a large box. Setting it on the kitchen table, she opened it up to display hundreds of snack cakes. Nothing, at all, but snack cakes. Ho-Ho's, Twinkies, Snowballs, Zingers, all in dozens of flavors and varieties.

She had spent every last penny we had in the world on the contents of that box, with nothing left over for even a gallon of milk to chug it down to.

And that is how I ended up eating nothing but snack cakes for a week. It's not a diet I'd recommend to anyone. Trust me on this one.

Compared to the Ho-Ho diet, the recipes I have in this section are downright wholesome. Okay, some of them may not be that great, but if you are broke, and/or have young children, they can be life savers.

Peanut Butter & Banana Sandwiches

- ✘ 1 banana
- ✘ peanut butter
- ✘ mayo

Mash up banana, add a few dollops of peanut butter (I prefer chunky) and a teaspoon of mayo. Mix and serve on either bread or toast.
Done.

☆☆☆☆☆☆☆☆☆☆☆☆☆☆☆☆☆☆☆☆☆☆☆☆☆☆☆☆☆☆☆☆☆☆☆☆

Notes:

Fried Baloney

- ✘ baloney
- ✘ cheese
- ✘ bread

In a skillet preheat on medium high.

While heating, take baloney and cut four equally distant lines, leaving the center untouched.
    *This keeps the baloney from curling, and forming a bubble in the middle while cooking.

Add a small dab of butter to skillet and when melted, throw on baloney.
When edges begin to curl, flip and add cheese.
Remove when melted, put on bread.
Done.

    *You can also do this with hotdogs. Just slice in half, fry, then add the cheese after it's been transferred to the bread.

☆ ☆

Notes:

Baloney Bowls

*   baloney

*   egg

*   cheese

*   cooking spray

In a sprayed cupcake baking dish, push baloney down to conform to cup.
Crack egg, and add to baloney.
Sprinkle with cheese.

Bake at 425 for about 10 to 15 minutes.
Done.

*You can add just about anything to this, tomato slices, diced onion, mushrooms, bacon bits, etc.

☆☆☆☆☆☆☆☆☆☆☆☆☆☆☆☆☆☆☆☆☆☆☆☆☆☆☆☆☆☆☆☆☆☆☆☆
Notes:

Hot Dog Wraps

- ✘ hot dogs
- ✘ cheese
- ✘ bacon
- ✘ buns

Take hot dogs out of package, slice halfway down, add cheese, then wrap in bacon.
Put in oven at 425 for about 10 to 15 minutes.
Put on buns.
Done.

   *If you buy cheese dogs you don't have to add it, just wrap it in bacon and bake.
OR
   *If you don't want to use bacon, you can wrap them up using a can of crescent rolls instead, and skip the buns. Helpful hint, start at the wide side of the triangle rolling towards the point, not the other way around.

☆☆☆☆☆☆☆☆☆☆☆☆☆☆☆☆☆☆☆☆☆☆☆☆☆☆☆☆☆☆☆☆☆☆☆☆☆
Notes:

Easy Chicken Fajita's

- ✘ 1 pre-cooked chicken patty (skinless works best, but any kind will do)
- ✘ 1 soft-shell tortilla
- ✘ shredded cheese

Optional:
- ✘ diced tomatoes
- ✘ diced onions or peppers
- ✘ green onions
- ✘ salsa
- ✘ sour cream (add afterward, not before you cook)

*You can make this in the oven or if you have a sandwich press that works as well (well, actually better, but you don't have to have one)

Slice the chicken on short side about into strips about the width of your pinky finger.

On one half of the tortilla add layer chicken
Sprinkle with cheese
Add any of the other ingredients if desired.

Fold tortilla in half and put in oven at 475 for 10 minutes
or in sandwich press for about 5 minutes
Done.

Notes:

Cold Tuna (or chicken) pasta salad

- ✘ 1 box of pasta (you can use shells, elbow or Rotini)
- ✘ 2 cans of tuna or 1 can of chicken
- ✘ 1 package of frozen peas
- ✘ 1 cup of mayo
- ✘ 1 packet of Ranch seasoning mix
- ✘ pepper

*I also like to add a teaspoon of horseradish to mine, but it's not necessary

Boil elbow macaroni and peas, for about 10 minutes, until macaroni is done.
Dump into colander and spray with cold water until macaroni has cooled off.
Drain, and put in big bowl.

Add undrained tuna or shredded chicken, mayo, Ranch packet and pepper to taste.
(If using chicken, shredded fresh carrots can be substituted for peas. DO NOT cook with pasta!)
Stir until everything is evenly mixed.

Refrigerate until chilled.
Done.

☆☆☆☆☆☆☆☆☆☆☆☆☆☆☆☆☆☆☆☆☆☆☆☆☆☆☆☆☆☆☆☆☆☆☆☆☆
Notes:

Tuna Melts

- ✗ 1 can of tuna (drained)
- ✗ mustard
- ✗ mayo
- ✗ dill relish
- ✗ pepper
- ✗ cheese slices

In a bowl mix tuna, a squirt of mustard, a dollop of mayo, a spoonful of dill relish & a sprinkling of pepper
Mix well
Spread on bread, add a slice of cheese

If you have a sandwich press:
Cook for around 5 minutes.
Done.

If you don't:
Heat up a skillet on medium heat
While waiting for skillet to heat up, butter bread
Place bread into skillet, add tuna mix & cheese, top with other slice of bread
Cook on each side around 5 minutes or until bread turns a golden brown.
Done.

*You can also add tomato or fresh baby spinach but **not** lettuce. Only bad can come from adding lettuce to a tuna melt while cooking.

☆☆☆☆☆☆☆☆☆☆☆☆☆☆☆☆☆☆☆☆☆☆☆☆☆☆☆☆☆☆☆☆☆☆☆☆☆☆☆
Notes:

Hamburger Pizza

- ✘ 1 – 2 lbs of hamburger (browned)
- ✘ ketchup, mustard, BBQ sauce (any kind)
- ✘ 1 finely diced onion
- ✘ American cheese slices
- ✘ buns (sandwich bread also works)

In a skillet brown hamburger with diced onion.
Drain grease and return to skillet.

Add an equal amount of ketchup, mustard and BBQ sauce.
Mix thoroughly.

Pull out buns, split in half and place on a baking sheet
Fill buns with hamburger mix
Add a cheese slice on top

Bake in oven at 350 until cheese is melted. About 10 - 15 minutes.
Done.

☆☆☆☆☆☆☆☆☆☆☆☆☆☆☆☆☆☆☆☆☆☆☆☆☆☆☆☆☆☆☆☆☆☆☆☆☆

Notes:

Open Faced Sandwiches

- ✗ 1 loaf of garlic bread
- ✗ 2 packages of cream cheese (softened)
- ✗ 4 packages of Budding lunchmeat (any kind)
- ✗ 1 diced tomato
- ✗ green onions (thinly sliced)

Place the garlic bread on a baking sheet
Layer lunchmeat evenly on both sides of the garlic bread

Spread cream cheese over the lunchmeat
Sprinkle with green onions & diced tomatoes

Bake in oven at 425 for 15 minutes.
Done.

*If you don't have garlic bread, you can use any kind of buns. Split in half, butter each side, and add a bit of garlic salt or powder.

*If you would rather, you can instead slice the lunchmeat into thin strips, and mix all the ingredients together with the cream cheese before spreading it over the bread. Either way is fine and they taste the same.

☆☆☆☆☆☆☆☆☆☆☆☆☆☆☆☆☆☆☆☆☆☆☆☆☆☆☆☆☆☆☆☆☆☆☆
Notes:

Poor Man's Brochette

- ✗ 1 loaf of garlic bread

- ✗ 2 cans of diced tomatoes (drained)

- ✗ shredded cheese (any kind, but I prefer to use a white cheese)

- ✗ Italian seasoning

Place garlic bread on a baking sheet.
Put an equal amount of diced tomatoes on each side of the garlic bread.
Sprinkle with shredded cheese & Italian seasoning

Bake in oven at 425 for 15 minutes.
Done.

☆☆☆☆☆☆☆☆☆☆☆☆☆☆☆☆☆☆☆☆☆☆☆☆☆☆☆☆☆☆☆☆☆☆

Notes:

<u>Chicken in a Basket</u>

- ✘ egg
- ✘ bread
- ✘ butter
- ✘ pepper

Take a slice of bread, and using a small glass remove a circle of bread.
Set circle aside.

Butter one side of bread.

Heat up small skillet to medium high.
Add a touch of butter to melt. Enough that it coats the bottom of the skillet.

Add bread butter side up & immediately crack egg in center of bread.
Add a dash of pepper

Cook a few minutes like you would for a sunny side up egg.
Then flip & cook about 1 – 2 minutes.

Remove from skillet, serve with bread circle.
Done.

☆☆☆☆☆☆☆☆☆☆☆☆☆☆☆☆☆☆☆☆☆☆☆☆☆☆☆☆☆☆☆☆☆☆☆☆☆☆☆

Notes:

Breakfast Rice

Okay, the amount of rice will depend on how many you are feeding. I'm going to give you the amounts for feeding four, but you can easily adjust this depending on how many you are cooking for.

- ✗ 2 cups of instant rice
- ✗ 2 cups of water
- ✗ handful of raisins (you can also add nuts, seeds or any other dehydrated fruit you like)
- ✗ 1 cup of milk
- ✗ 1 cup of sugar
- ✗ cinnamon

Bring water to boil and add rice and raisins.
Remove from heat and let set until water is absorbed.
Then add milk, sugar and a sprinkling of cinnamon, and stir.
Done.

☆☆☆☆☆☆☆☆☆☆☆☆☆☆☆☆☆☆☆☆☆☆☆☆☆☆☆☆☆☆☆☆☆☆☆☆☆

Notes:

Grits 'n Smokies

This is easily adjustable to feed 1 or more people.

- ✘ instant grits
- ✘ Little Smokies
- ✘ shredded cheese (any kind you like)

Following the directions for grits on the box, add the Little Smokies to your water while bring it to a boil.
Add grits to the boiling water, cook according to directions.
Once all the water has been absorbed, add a handful of cheese.
Done.

Notes:

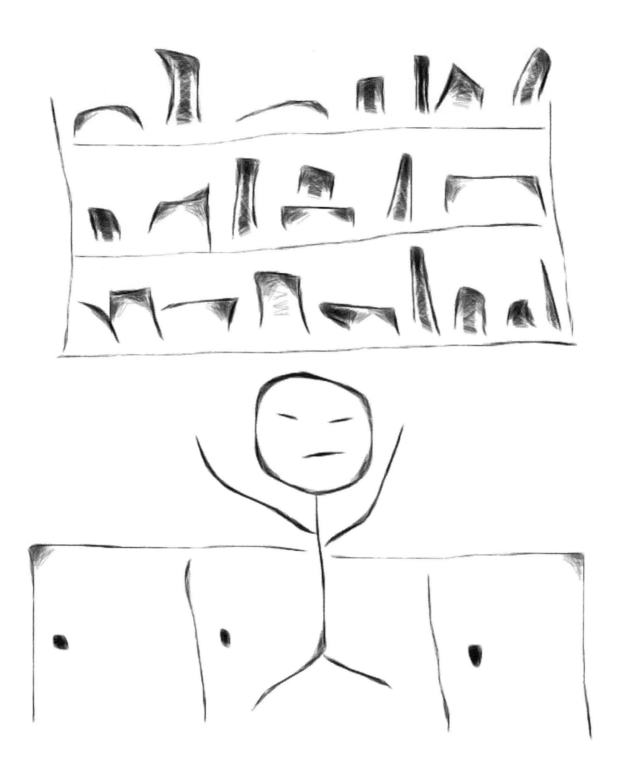

"Food is an important part of a balanced diet."

- Fran Lebowitz

 Simple Sides

I remember the first pie I ever made that didn't come from the frozen food section. It was a cherry pie, and I was so proud of myself. I had been given a quart of fresh cherries by a neighbor, in exchange for sewing a few lost buttons back on his shirt and I decided that I would try my hand at baking a pie. Completely from scratch.

It was a beautiful pie, with a basket weave top, lightly sprinkled with a butter and sugar coating. It had turned out just like the photo they showed in the cookbook, and I couldn't have been happier.

Lightly wrapping the pie up in cheesecloth before going to bed, I left it on the stove with plans to serve it at dinner the following day.

Opening my bedroom door the next morning, I noticed a smell, but couldn't put my finger on what it was. It didn't smell bad per se, it smelled thick and vaguely sticky, and I was at a complete loss as to what it could be. Poking around the living room, I realized the odor was stronger near the kitchen. Following my nose, I wandered through my kitchen sniffing the air, finally stopping before my stove. Putting my hand on it to lean down I quickly snatched my hand away realizing it was hot. Blowing on my fingers, I opened the oven with the other hand and was greeted by the smell of... of... something.

Grabbing the oven mitts, I reached in, and pulled out a round pie pan, with a black, bubbling tar-like center that once, that not so many hours ago, had been my beautiful pie! Dropping the oozing mess onto the top of the stove with a loud *clang!* I gave out a short wail of distress.

In response to my wail, the bedroom door opened and my husband stepped through with a sheepish grin on his face. "Oh yeah. I forgot about that. I saw the pie when I came home last night and put it in the oven to warm up. But I guess I forgot about it after my shower and went to bed. Sorry about that."

I didn't even get a taste of the first pie I ever made. After warming in the oven for over 6 hours it was an unsalvageable mess that had to be thrown away, pie pan and all. Once it was cooled down enough to safely throw away, the pie had hardened into something that more resembled asphalt than the cherry pie I'd been so proud of.

I'll admit it, I cried a little bit.

Oven Roasted Potatoes

- ✘ potatoes
- ✘ 1 packet of Lipton's garlic & herb seasoning
- ✘ olive oil

Wash and cube potatoes, then put them all in a big ziplock bag.

*I always leave the skins on because, A) I'm lazy and B) it's the most nutritious part of the potato

Add enough olive oil to coat them, then add 1 packet of Lipton's garlic & herb seasoning. Shake well then pour into greased pan.

Bake in the oven for about 30 minutes at 450.
Done.

*You know their done with a fork slides easily into the potato.

☆☆☆☆☆☆☆☆☆☆☆☆☆☆☆☆☆☆☆☆☆☆☆☆☆☆☆☆☆☆☆☆☆☆

Notes:

Potatoes & Green Beans

- ✗ potatoes (washed and cubed)
- ✗ 1 bag of frozen green beans (this is also good with corn)
- ✗ 1 diced onion
- ✗ 1 stick of real butter (sliced into thin squares or you can melt it in the microwave for 1 minute)
- ✗ 1 packet of Lipton garlic & herb seasoning (optional)

In a baking dish, add all of the ingredients, stir thoroughly. If you decided not to microwave the butter, add evenly on top.

Bake uncovered at 450 for about 30 - 45 minutes depending on big your potato cubes are. Done.

*Potatoes are done when a fork can slide in easily.

☆☆☆☆☆☆☆☆☆☆☆☆☆☆☆☆☆☆☆☆☆☆☆☆☆☆☆☆☆☆☆☆☆☆☆☆
Notes:

Radish & Carrots

Okay, believe it or not, my kids actually do like this. Try it for yourself, who knows, you might be pleasantly surprised.

- ✘ Either one bag of frozen carrots OR one bag of baby carrots
- ✘ 1 bunch of radishes, washed & cubed
- ✘ olive oil
- ✘ 1/2 a stick of real butter

Put all ingredients in a baking dish, then drizzle with olive oil.
You can either cook this in the microwave for 5 - 7 minutes, pausing at 3 minutes to stir.

OR

Bake in the oven at 400 for around 30 minutes. Again, taking out around the midway mark to stir all the ingredients.
Done.

*Veggies are done when your fork easily slides inside the radishes.

☆ ☆
Notes:

Honeyed Carrots

Honeyed carrots goes over well with my kids and are easy to make.

- ✗ 1 package of frozen carrots
- ✗ A half a stick of butter
- ✗ honey

Pour carrots into a microwave safe dish.

Slice up butter and place evenly over the carrots, then drizzle honey over the top.

Microwave for about 3 minutes, remove and stir and cook again for another 2 - 5 minutes depending on the wattage of your microwave.
Done.

☆ ☆

Notes:

Apple Salad

- ✗ 6 red apples (cubed)
- ✗ 1 bag of walnuts
- ✗ 1 bag of carrots (shredded)
- ✗ 1 cup of raisins
- ✗ 1 cup of mayo

In a big mixing bowl dump all the ingredients in, add the mayo and stir well, evenly coating everything. If there isn't enough mayo to cover everything completely add a bit more.

Chill.

☆ ☆

Notes:

Potato Salad

- ✗ 1 bag of potatoes, diced
- ✗ 3 hard boiled eggs, diced
- ✗ 1 finely diced onion
- ✗ mayo & mustard, paprika & pepper

Put diced potatoes in a pot, cover in water and bring to a boil.

After reaching a boil, continue to cook for another 10 minutes or until fork slides in potato but not mushy.
Drain and put in bowl & refrigerate overnight.

The next day add mayo, mustard, onion, diced egg and spices. Mix well.
Garnish with a sprinkling of paprika before serving.
Done.

☆☆☆☆☆☆☆☆☆☆☆☆☆☆☆☆☆☆☆☆☆☆☆☆☆☆☆☆☆☆☆☆☆☆☆☆☆

Notes:

Ranch Pasta Salad

- ✗ 1 box of either shell, elbow or rotini cooked according to box directions
- ✗ 1 bag of frozen peas
- ✗ 1 bag of fresh carrots (shred)
- ✗ 1 cup of mayo (can add more if needed)
- ✗ 1 packet of Ranch seasoning mix

Boil pasta & peas.
Drain.

When chilled, add mayo, ranch and carrots.
Refrigerate until ready to serve.
Done.

*Can quickly be turned into a meal by adding either of the following:
- ✗ tuna
- ✗ canned chicken

☆☆☆☆☆☆☆☆☆☆☆☆☆☆☆☆☆☆☆☆☆☆☆☆☆☆☆☆☆☆☆☆☆☆☆☆☆☆

Notes:

Vegetable Pasta

- ✗ 1 box of angel hair pasta
- ✗ 1 stick of butter
- ✗ 1 bag of mixed veggies (I prefer to use the stir fry mix, but any kind you like will work)
- ✗ garlic, dill and oregano work well with this or Lipton's garlic & herb mix

Cook pasta according to directions, add the vegetables when you add the pasta.
Drain and put back on stove.
Add butter and spices, stirring until butter is melted.
Remove from heat. Serve.

OR

Instead of cooking the vegetables with the pasta, while the pasta is boiling you can saute the vegetables in a skillet on medium high.
Melt a stick of butter, add spices and vegetables and cook for around 5 minutes or until they are thoroughly cooked but not limp.
When everything is done, mix together in a mixing bowl.
Done.

   *This can be quickly turned into a meal by adding either of these:
   - ✗ tuna
   - ✗ canned chicken

☆☆☆☆☆☆☆☆☆☆☆☆☆☆☆☆☆☆☆☆☆☆☆☆☆☆☆☆☆☆☆☆☆☆☆☆☆☆☆
Notes:

Italian Vegetable Pasta

- ✗ 1 box of angel hair pasta
- ✗ Italian dressing
- ✗ 1 bag of mixed veggies (I prefer to use the stirfry mix, but any kind you like will work)

Cook pasta according to directions, add the vegetables when you add the pasta. Drain and put back on stove.
Add enough Italian dressing to cover pasta without drowning them.
Remove from heat.
Done.

OR

You can serve this as a cold side dish. Instead of putting it back on the stove, rinse in cold water until cool to the touch. Put in serving bowl and add Italian dressing.

OR

If you are not big on the taste of Italian dressing you can substitute olive oil and add your own spices. For this I'd recommend garlic, dill and oregano.

*Can quickly be turned into a meal by adding either of the following:
- ✗ tuna
- ✗ canned chicken

☆☆☆
Notes:

Mac & Cheese

- ✗ 1 box of shell macaroni
- ✗ 1 box of Velveeta cheese
- ✗ 2 cups of milk
- ✗ 1 stick of real butter
- ✗ pepper & garlic

Cook pasta according to directions.
In another pot placed cubed Velveeta, butter and milk.
On low melt cheese mixture. Add spices when melted. Stir.

In a sprayed baking dish, add macaroni, then stir in cheese until all the pasta is covered.
Bake in oven at 350 for a half hour.

You can also make this in the crock pot. Cook your pasta, drain and put in crock pot.
Add milk, cubed Velveeta cheese, butter and spices.
Cook on low for around 4 - 6 hours, stirring occasionally.

*If you want to make this into a meal, you can add any of the following:
- ✗ little smokies
- ✗ sliced hot dogs
- ✗ 1 lb browned hamburger
- ✗ 1 drained can of tuna

(honestly, any kind of meat will work but these are the simplest)

☆☆

Notes:

Cheesy Hashbrowns

* ✗ 1 bag of shredded frozen hashbrowns (or you can use Potatoes O'Brian)
* ✗ 2 cans of cheese soup (or you can use shredded cheese, just add a slick of melted butter if you do)
* ✗ spice to taste
* ✗ cooking spray

Cover baking dish with cooking spray.
Dump in hasbrowns and cheese soup.
Add your spices, then mix thoroughly.

Bake uncovered in oven at 450 for around 30 minutes.

You can also use Velveeta cheese. Just follow the directions from the Mac & Cheese recipe, substituting the hashbrowns for pasta.

*Can quickly be turned into a meal by adding any of the following:
* ✗ browned hamburger or sausage
* ✗ Little Smokies
* ✗ sliced Kielbasa

☆ ☆

Notes:

Cheesy Corn

- ✗ 1 bag of frozen corn
- ✗ 1 cup of shredded cheese (can also use Velveeta)
- ✗ 1 slick of real butter (sliced)

Put everything into a baking dish.
Add pepper if desired.

Bake at 350 for 30 minutes.
Stir about halfway through.
Done.

*You can also throw this into the microwave for about 5 to 10 minutes depending on how powerful your microwave is.

☆☆☆☆☆☆☆☆☆☆☆☆☆☆☆☆☆☆☆☆☆☆☆☆☆☆☆☆☆☆☆☆☆☆☆☆☆☆☆

Notes:

Mushroom Rice

- ✗ 1 cup of instant rice
- ✗ 1 can of cream of mushroom soup
- ✗ I can of mushrooms
- ✗ 1/2 a cup of milk
- ✗ Lowery's seasoning salt

Pour uncooked rice into an 8x8 greased baking dish until it covers the bottom.
Add cream of mushroom soup, undrained mushrooms, milk and seasoning salt.
Stir thoroughly.

Bake uncovered at 450 for about 30 minutes.
Done.

*Can quickly be made into a meal by adding browned hamburger.

Notes:

Garlic Rice

- ✗ instant rice
- ✗ 1 stick of butter
- ✗ garlic (you can either use fresh minced garlic or you can use garlic powder)

Make rice according to directions.
Remove from heat, stir and cover.

When water has been completely absorbed, add butter and garlic to taste, and simmer on low heat until the butter is completely melted.
Done.

*Can be quickly made into a meal by adding any of the following:
- ✗ tuna & peas
- ✗ canned chicken & sliced carrots
- ✗ Little Smokies & stir fly veggies
- ✗ sliced kielbasa & stir fry veggies
- ✗ browned hamburger & mushrooms

☆☆☆☆☆☆☆☆☆☆☆☆☆☆☆☆☆☆☆☆☆☆☆☆☆☆☆☆☆☆☆☆☆☆☆☆☆

Notes:

Chicken Rice

- ✗ 1 cup of instant rice
- ✗ 1 can of cream of chicken soup
- ✗ 1/2 a cup of milk
- ✗ 1 package of Lipton's garlic & herb seasoning
- ✗ Optional: carrots, either frozen or canned can be added.

Pour uncooked rice into a 8x8 greased baking dish.
Add cream of chicken soup, *carrots, milk and seasoning salt.
Stir thoroughly.

Bake uncovered at 450 for about 30 minutes.
Done.

   *Can be quickly turned into a meal by adding a can of shredded chicken and carrots, either frozen or canned.

☆☆☆☆☆☆☆☆☆☆☆☆☆☆☆☆☆☆☆☆☆☆☆☆☆☆☆☆☆☆☆☆☆☆☆
Notes:

Mexican Rice

- ✗ instant rice
- ✗ 1- 2 cans of diced tomatoes
- ✗ chili power & pepper to taste
- ✗ 1 can chili beans (optional)
- ✗ 1 bag shredded cheese (optional)
- ✗ frozen mixed peppers (optional)

Make rice according to directions.
Remove from heat, stir and cover.

When water is completely absorbed, add tomatoes, chili beans, chili powers, pepper and cheese.
Return to low heat, stirring until either beans are warm or cheese is melted (if you added cheese).

*Can quickly be made into a meal by adding any of the following:
- ✗ hamburger
- ✗ sliced hot dogs
- ✗ Little Smokies
- ✗ sliced Kielbasa

☆☆☆☆☆☆☆☆☆☆☆☆☆☆☆☆☆☆☆☆☆☆☆☆☆☆☆☆☆☆☆☆☆☆☆☆☆☆
Notes:

Cheesy Rice

- ✗ instant rice
- ✗ 1 bag of shredded cheese or can of cheese soup
- ✗ pepper, garlic, dill and oregano works well with this

Make rice according to directions.
Remove from heat, stir and cover.

When water has been completely absorbed, add cheese and spices.
Simmer on low heat until the cheese is completely melted.
Done.

*Can be quickly made into a meal by adding any of the following:
- ✗ tuna
- ✗ Kielbasa
- ✗ sliced hot dogs
- ✗ Little Smokies

☆ ☆

Notes:

<u>Pickle Wraps</u>

- ✘ Pickle spears
- ✘ 1 package of ham deli meat
- ✘ 1 block of softened cream cheese
- ✘ Ranch seasoning mix

Mix cream cheese & ranch together in a small bowl.

Take 1 slice of ham, spread with a layer of cream cheese mix.
Place pickle on one side, roll tightly.

Slice into bite sized pieces.
Done.

☆☆☆☆☆☆☆☆☆☆☆☆☆☆☆☆☆☆☆☆☆☆☆☆☆☆☆☆☆☆☆☆☆☆
Notes:

Cream Cheese Spreads

Cream cheese is versatile, easy to work with (once its reached room temperature) and can substitute as an actual meal on a lazy afternoon. Here are a few of my favorites, but don't be afraid to get creative, you can throw almost anything into cream cheese, and have a pretty amazing cracker meal.

Filling Options:

2 pickle spears - 1 package cut up Budding ham

1 small package of imitation crab meat - green onions

1 package cut up Budding ham - green onions

1 diced up jalapeno (make sure to get rid of all the seeds) - bacon bits

1 packet of Lipton's garlic & herb dried soup mix

1 packet ranch dressing mix - 1 pickle spear - 1 package cut up Budding ham

1 packet ranch dressing mix - bacon bits

Directions:

In a mixing bowl add cream cheese and the rest of your ingredients on top.
Using a wooden spoon, mix until everything is evenly distributed.
(Full disclosure, sometimes I use my hands to mix it. It's faster, but it is messier.)
Grab your favorite cracker and eat.

☆☆☆☆☆☆☆☆☆☆☆☆☆☆☆☆☆☆☆☆☆☆☆☆☆☆☆☆☆☆☆☆☆☆

Notes:

"If more of us valued food and cheer and song above hoarded gold, it would be a merrier world."

- J.R.R. Tolkien

Holiday Meals

I enjoy cooking exactly three times a year, Easter, Thanksgiving, and Christmas. Which is why you will only see these three meals talked about in the Holiday Meals. Yes, there are other holiday's in which you can make big meals, 4th of July comes to mind, or maybe an intimate dinner for two on Valentine's Day, but year in, and year out, it is these big three that I look forward to.

It's not just the food, which I make a lot of. It's opening my doors to anyone who wants to enjoy good food and good company, having people streaming through my doors, the shouts of cheer and the echoes of laughter running through my house that makes these holidays special for me. Rarely do I know how many will be there. Every person living in my house is welcome to invite whoever they want, and most do. And everyone who knows me, knows that invited or not, they are welcome to join our celebration, and many have. My home during the holidays is often a refuge for the lonely, the displaced, and anyone who wants a place to feel welcome.

I love the noise and the general chaos that these holiday meals bring into my house. There's no actual set tradition for any of them, there have been years when boardgames have been pulled out, and others where beer pong has ruled the day. We've had silly string fights over Easter, and Doctor Who marathons over Christmas. The only important part is that we are there together, having fun.

I am giving you the entire holiday meal menu, grouped together as I make them. Obviously, you are free to add, subtract or modify any meal here that you plan on making. And, like all the recipes in this book, they are as simple and easy as I can make them. Most can be prepared ahead of time, leaving you time to enjoy the day, rather than stuck in the kitchen while everyone else is relaxing. I usually make everything the day before, pulling each thing out of the fridge as it needs to be cooked and popping it directly into the oven. It helps make the holidays stress free and keeps my kitchen clean, all at the same time.

One last bit of advice. I always purchase cooking tins for everything I make, that way when we are done eating, instead of being consigned to scrubbing a mountain of dirty dishes, they can be easily thrown away. Paper plates and plastic silverware also rule the day, because taking out a full trash bag is so much easier than washing dishes for twenty or more people.

"After a good dinner one can forgive anybody, even one's own relations."

-Oscar Wilde

Easter Dinner

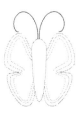

Around my house, Easter dinner is also a time to celebrate spring so I like to make new spring foods, salads, and pasta. When the weather is nice we'll even BBQ the ham on the grill and eat outside picnic style.

Ham

- ✘ 1 holiday ham
- ✘ 1 cup of brown sugar
- ✘ 1 can of crushed pineapple
- ✘ 1 bottle of BBQ sauce (any kind that you like that's a bit sweet)
- ✘ tin foil

Mix brown sugar, pineapple & BBQ sauce together
Pull out enough tin foil to wrap your ham up then place in baking container.
Put ham in baking dish, then cover with mix.
Wrap up tin foil.

Bake at 325 pulling out periodically to baste with mix that's now at the bottom of the baking dish.

Follow directions on ham for time needed to fully cook.
   *You can also make this on the grill like I mentioned before. Get a good slow burning fire going and keep it steady around 350. You'll need to baste it more often than in the oven but I think the smoke add a nice flavor.

Potato Salad

- ✗ 1 bag of potatoes, diced
- ✗ 3 hard boiled eggs, diced
- ✗ 1 finely diced onion
- ✗ mayo & mustard, paprika & pepper

Put diced potatoes in a pot, cover in water and bring to a boil.

After reaching a boil, continue to cook for another 10 minutes or until fork slides in potato but not mushy.
Drain and put in bowl & refrigerate overnight.

The next day add mayo, mustard, onion, diced egg and spices. Mix well.
Garnish with a sprinkling of paprika before serving.

Ranch Pasta Salad

- ✗ 1 box of either shell, elbow or rotini cooked according to box directions
- ✗ 1 bag of frozen peas
- ✗ 1 bag of fresh carrots (shred)
- ✗ 1 cup of mayo (can add more if needed)
- ✗ 1 packet of Ranch seasoning mix

Boil pasta & peas.
Drain.
When chilled, add mayo, ranch and carrots.
Refrigerate until ready to serve.

Apple Salad

- ✗ 6 red apples (cubed)
- ✗ 1 bag of walnuts
- ✗ 1 bag of carrots (shredded)
- ✗ 1 cup of raisins
- ✗ 1 cup of mayo

In a big mixing bowl dump all the ingredients in, add the mayo and stir well, evenly coating everything.
If there isn't enough mayo to cover everything completely add a bit more.
Chill.

Coleslaw

- ✗ 1 cup of Miracle Whip (not mayo)
- ✗ 1/2 cup of sugar
- ✗ 3 tablespoons of vegetable oil
- ✗ 3 teaspoons apple cider vinegar
- ✗ 1/2 teaspoon celery salt
- ✗ 8 cups of cabbage (finely chopped)
- ✗ 2 medium carrots (shredded)
- ✗ 1 onion (diced)

*I generally throw my cabbage, carrots and onion in a food processor, but you can also do it by hand

In a large bowl mix sugar, vegetable oil and vinegar.
Add onions, celery salt, cabbage and carrots.
Add miracle whip and stir thoroughly.
Refrigerate overnight (24 hours even better, but at least overnight)

Deviled Eggs

- ✗ a dozen eggs
- ✗ mayo
- ✗ mustard
- ✗ paprika

Submerge eggs in a pot of water.
Bring eggs to a boil. Continue boiling for around 10 minutes.
Drain and cool. Either over night in the refrigerator or by submerging in cold water.

When cool remove shells & cut in half.
Remove yokes, mash & mix with mayo and mustard until creamy.
Dollop back into egg, garnish with paprika.

Fruit Crisp

- ✗ 1 big bag of frozen fruit (you can also use fresh fruit as well)
- ✗ 2 cups of oatmeal
- ✗ 1 cup of sugar
- ✗ 1/2 cup of brown sugar
- ✗ a few good shakes of cinnamon
- ✗ and a dash of vanilla
- ✗ 1 stick of melted butter
- ✗ cooking spray

Coat a baking dish with the nonstick spray.
Pour thawed fruit into the baking dish.

In a mixing bowl combine oatmeal, sugar, brown sugar, cinnamon and vanilla. Stir well.
Evenly coat the top of the fruit with the oatmeal mix.
Pour melted butter over everything.
Bake at 350 for a half hour.

"I come from a family where gravy is considered a beverage."
-Erma Bombeck

 # Thanksgiving Dinner

I love Thanksgiving. I love all the food, the not having to buy gifts, the company, and comfort of this holiday. These foods are all what I consider "comfort" foods, warm, heavy, and sleep inducing. Everything to get you ready for the long winter hibernation.

Turkey

* ✖ 1 turkey
* ✖ 1 stick of real butter
* ✖ salt

The night before put thawed turkey in a large pot filled with water, ¼ of a cup of salt and other spices that you might like. Garlic, dill and oregano are good choices, but not necessary.

The next day, take turkey and put into roasting pan, breast side up. Coat with a light layer of salt, rub completely in. Do this two or three times.

Do NOT forget to dig out the giblets and neck that they stuff inside the turkey. I've done it and it's a bad idea.

Put in oven, covered. Every hour remove turkey and baste with real butter.

I believe the general cooking time is 1 hour for every four pounds of turkey, cooked at 325. But follow directions on turkey wrapper if it says differently.

When there are enough drippings at the bottom, use that to baste the turkey with. Uncover the last hour to brown.

Little Smokies

- 2 packages of little smokes
- 1 jar of grape jelly
- 1 jar shrimp sauce

Throw everything into crock pot.
Wait 4 hours.
Stir on occasion.

Homemade Mac & Cheese

- 1 box of shell macaroni (or you can use any kind of short pasta you like)
- 1 box of Velveeta cheese
- 2 cups of milk
- 1 stick of real butter
- pepper & garlic

Cook pasta according to directions.

In another pot placed cubed Velveeta, butter and milk.
On low melt cheese mixture. Add spices when melted. Stir.

In a sprayed baking dish, add macaroni, then stir in cheese until all the pasta is covered.
Bake in oven at 350 for a half hour.

Stuffing

Buy a box of Stovetop stuffing. Use drippings from turkey instead of butter and water. Cook according to box directions.
   *Trust me, it's better this way

Green Bean Casserole

- ✘ 4 cans of french cut green beans (drained)
- ✘ 2 cans of cream of mushroom soup
- ✘ 1 container of french onions
- ✘ pepper & Lowery's seasoning salt to taste

In a sprayed baking dish, mix together all the ingredients except the french onions.
Smooth top, then sprinkle the french onions on top.
Bake at 350 for half hour.

Party Potatoes

- ✘ 1 bag of potatoes, diced
- ✘ 1 container of sour cream
- ✘ 1 stick of real butter
- ✘ ½ cup of milk
- ✘ 1 bunch of green onions
- ✘ 1 bag of any kind of shredded cheese
- ✘ salt & pepper to taste

Boil potatoes until a fork can easily slide in. Drain and put in large mixing bowl.
While potatoes are boiling, finely slice green onions.

Add all the rest of the ingredients except the cheese & onions to your potatoes.
Using a mixer, thoroughly blend until creamy.

Add ½ of the cheese & onions, mix again until evenly distributed.
Pour into a sprayed baking dish, cover top with remaining cheese.
Bake at 350 for half an hour.

Cheesy Corn

- ✘ 1 bag of frozen corn
- ✘ 1 cup of shredded cheese
- ✘ 1 slick of real butter (sliced)

Put everything into a baking dish, add pepper if desired.
Bake at 350 for 30 minutes, stir about halfway through.

*You can also throw this into the microwave for about 5 to 10 minutes depending on how powerful your microwave is.

Rolls

Buy packaged rolls from store.

Put on cookie sheet.

Baste top with drippings from turkey.

Cook according to directions.

Fill out the rest of the meal with things like:

Veggie Platter

Cheese, summer sausage & cracker platter

& those pickle wraps make a nice addition as well

Add a couple of pies (you're on your own there) and you're set!

"Food is our common ground, a universal experience."

- James Beard

Christmas Brunch

Christmas morning shouldn't be about slaving over a hot stove. It should be about relaxing, opening presents and spending time with family and friends. Which is why this is the perfect meal for doing all of that, since you make it up the day before and only have to shove it into the oven when you wake up.

Heart Attack Casserole

- ✗ A dozen eggs
- ✗ sour cream
- ✗ a bunch of green onions
- ✗ 1 lb sausage (browned & drained)
- ✗ a jar of mushrooms
- ✗ ½ a loaf of bread
- ✗ 1 package of shredded cheese
- ✗ 1 stick of real butter
- ✗ salt, pepper, garlic & dill
- ✗ 1 bag of the cheapest, greasiest plain potato chips you can find that are tasty

In a sprayed baking dish, layer to bottom completely with bread. Add cooked sausage, mushrooms, onions & cheese.

In a mixing bowl, combine eggs, sour cream & spices. Mix well. Pour into baking dish.

Cover and put in refrigerator overnight.

The next morning:

Put casserole in oven at 350 for about 2 (sometimes 3) hours.

When egg casserole is setting up but not yet done, with about 30 minutes left to cook, take out of oven, add one bag of completely crushed potato chips and pour 1 stick of melted butter over the top.

Put back in oven and continue to cook until a knife comes out clean when stuck in the middle.

*Serve with cookies, eggnog, wine, or whatever makes you happy on Christmas morning.

While the casserole is cooking, open presents and enjoy time with your family & friends who have come to share Christmas morning with you!

Do NOTHING else the rest of the day (except watch A Christmas Story, that's a must do!) that doesn't make you happy.

"My dishwasher has two modes... dangerously overfull or my favorite coffee mug."

-Ron Hammerquest

 # In a Pinch

We've all been there, we're getting ready to make dinner thinking we have everything we need, and then realize, nope. So now we have three choices:

1 - we can stop everything and run to the store

2 - we can scrape the entire meal and hope something else will present itself

OR

3 - look to a valid substitution

If you've decided to go with option 3, I've made a quick list of things you can substitute for basic ingredients. And feel free to write in the margins if you come across any I didn't list here.

I've also added a few food modifications I've discovered over the years that you might enjoy, a couple of helpful tips if you've made a mistake on how you can fix it, and some quick cheats to make mealtime even faster with less fuss.

Substitutions

→ If you don't have an egg, you can use 2 tablespoons of vegetable oil instead

→ If you are out of milk, you can use:

    ✗ powered creamer (¼ powder for every cup of milk)

    ✗ or evaporated milk (mix half & half)

    ✗ or for anything that isn't sweet use sour cream

→ If a recipe calls for tomato soup and you don't have any, you can use ketchup (and vice versa)

➔ Powdered sugar can be used instead of granulated sugar, but increase the amount by a third. You can also use honey, but cut back by a third.

➔ If you're out of mayonnaise you can use sour cream or yogurt

➔ If you're out of unsweetened cocoa, you can use powdered hot cocoa mix just cut back on the sugar 1 for 1. So if it calls for 1 tablespoon of cocoa, cut back 1 tablespoon of sugar.

➔ If a recipe calls for chicken or beef broth, bullion cubes are always an acceptable substitution.

➔ If you're out of unsalted butter you can use shorting instead.

Modifications

➔ Canned fruit can be added to any cake mix but make sure they match each other:

  ✗ chocolate cake: cherries or strawberries

  ✗ yellow cake: pineapple or strawberry

  ✗ pink cake: cherries or strawberries

➔ For creamier pudding, use instant powdered milk (make it slightly thicker than the recipe calls for on the box)

➔ For richer box Mac & Cheese use sour cream instead of milk

➔ For richer chocolate cake add 1 cup of real mayo to your recipe

Salvaging a Mistake

➔ If you have added too much of a hot spice to a recipe and it burns when you taste it, you can add honey to tone it down.

➔ If you've added to much salt to a sauce based meal, put it a raw potato to help absorb the salt, and add an extra cup of water to help thin it out.

➔ If you've made a meal too sweet, you can add a dash of apple cider vinegar or lemon juice to balance out the taste.

Quick Cheats

→ If you are making french toast and need a lot of it, you can bake it in the oven instead of on the stove. Use a baking sheet, and don't forget the non-stick cooking spray. Cook at 400 for about 10 - 15 minutes.

→ You can also do this with grilled cheese, just flip it after about 5 -7 minutes.

→ You can also make bacon in the oven. Use a broiling pan (it's a metal baking dish with slots on top that comes in two pieces). Just lay bacon on top, and bake for around 10 minutes or so depending on how crispy you want your bacon. The grease falls down into the baking dish below so it's already pre-drained and doesn't need to blot it with a paper towel or napkin when finished.

→ Anything you boil can also be made in a pressure cooker. Just remember when making anything in a pressure cooker, you need to cut the normal cooking time in half.

→ If your kids aren't big on eating their veggies and it's a battle to the death to get them to eat them, this might help. When making almost any kind of pasta dish or anything with a tomato base, buy a bag of frozen veggies (almost any kind will do) and run it through a food processor (while still frozen) until they are thoroughly minced. Add them to your meal and your kids will never notice to complain.

→ Delivery is always an option :)

And remember cooking isn't a science, it's an adventure where failure is always an option. So have fun, and keep a frozen pizza in the freezer in case things don't work out.

My favorite recipes

Recipe:_____

Created by: _____

☆☆☆☆☆☆☆☆☆☆☆☆☆☆☆☆☆

Ingredients:

☆☆☆☆☆☆☆☆☆☆☆☆☆☆☆☆☆

Directions:

Recipe:_____

Created by: _____

☆☆☆☆☆☆☆☆☆☆☆☆☆☆☆☆☆☆

Ingredients:

☆☆☆☆☆☆☆☆☆☆☆☆☆☆☆☆☆☆

Directions:

Recipe:_____

Created by: _____

☆☆☆☆☆☆☆☆☆☆☆☆☆☆☆☆☆☆

Ingredients:

☆☆☆☆☆☆☆☆☆☆☆☆☆☆☆☆☆☆

Directions:

Recipe:_____

Created by: _____

☆☆☆☆☆☆☆☆☆☆☆☆☆☆☆☆☆☆☆

Ingredients:

☆☆☆☆☆☆☆☆☆☆☆☆☆☆☆☆☆☆☆

Directions:

Recipe:_____

Created by: _____

☆☆☆☆☆☆☆☆☆☆☆☆☆☆☆☆☆☆☆☆

Ingredients:

☆☆☆☆☆☆☆☆☆☆☆☆☆☆☆☆☆☆☆☆

Directions:

Recipe:_____

Created by: _____

☆☆☆☆☆☆☆☆☆☆☆☆☆☆☆☆☆☆

Ingredients:

☆☆☆☆☆☆☆☆☆☆☆☆☆☆☆☆☆☆

Directions:

Recipe:_____

Created by: _____ 🙂

☆☆☆☆☆☆☆☆☆☆☆☆☆☆☆☆☆☆

Ingredients:

☆☆☆☆☆☆☆☆☆☆☆☆☆☆☆☆☆☆

Directions:

Recipe:_____ 🙂

Created by: _____

☆☆☆☆☆☆☆☆☆☆☆☆☆☆☆☆☆☆

Ingredients:

☆☆☆☆☆☆☆☆☆☆☆☆☆☆☆☆☆☆

Directions:

Recipe:_____

Created by: _____

☆☆☆☆☆☆☆☆☆☆☆☆☆☆☆☆☆☆

Ingredients:

☆☆☆☆☆☆☆☆☆☆☆☆☆☆☆☆☆☆

Directions:

Recipe:_____

Created by: _____

☆☆☆☆☆☆☆☆☆☆☆☆☆☆☆☆☆☆

Ingredients:

☆☆☆☆☆☆☆☆☆☆☆☆☆☆☆☆☆☆

Directions:

Recipe:_____

Created by: _____

☆☆☆☆☆☆☆☆☆☆☆☆☆☆☆☆☆☆

Ingredients:

☆☆☆☆☆☆☆☆☆☆☆☆☆☆☆☆☆☆

Directions:

Recipe:_____

Created by: _____

☆☆☆☆☆☆☆☆☆☆☆☆☆☆☆☆☆☆

Ingredients:

☆☆☆☆☆☆☆☆☆☆☆☆☆☆☆☆☆☆

Directions:

Recipe:_____

Created by: _____

☆☆☆☆☆☆☆☆☆☆☆☆☆☆☆☆☆☆

Ingredients:

☆☆☆☆☆☆☆☆☆☆☆☆☆☆☆☆☆☆

Directions:

Recipe:_____

Created by: _____

☆☆☆☆☆☆☆☆☆☆☆☆☆☆☆☆☆☆

Ingredients:

☆☆☆☆☆☆☆☆☆☆☆☆☆☆☆☆☆☆

Directions:

Recipe:_____

Created by: _____

☆☆☆☆☆☆☆☆☆☆☆☆☆☆☆☆☆

Ingredients:

☆☆☆☆☆☆☆☆☆☆☆☆☆☆☆☆☆

Directions:

Recipe:_____

Created by: _____

☆☆☆☆☆☆☆☆☆☆☆☆☆☆☆☆☆☆☆☆

Ingredients:

☆☆☆☆☆☆☆☆☆☆☆☆☆☆☆☆☆☆☆☆

Directions:

Recipe:_____

Created by: _____

☆☆☆☆☆☆☆☆☆☆☆☆☆☆☆☆☆☆

Ingredients:

☆☆☆☆☆☆☆☆☆☆☆☆☆☆☆☆☆☆

Directions:

Recipe:_____

Created by: _____

☆☆☆☆☆☆☆☆☆☆☆☆☆☆☆☆☆☆

Ingredients:

☆☆☆☆☆☆☆☆☆☆☆☆☆☆☆☆☆☆

Directions:

Recipe:_____ ☺

Created by: _____

☆ ☆ ☆ ☆ ☆ ☆ ☆ ☆ ☆ ☆ ☆ ☆ ☆ ☆ ☆ ☆ ☆ ☆

Ingredients:

☆ ☆ ☆ ☆ ☆ ☆ ☆ ☆ ☆ ☆ ☆ ☆ ☆ ☆ ☆ ☆ ☆ ☆

Directions:

If you enjoyed this cookbook , please
consider leaving a review on GoodReads.
You can use the QR code below to take
you directly there.

To follow more of Lisa's misadventures in living visit her website at: http://pandra411.wixsite.com/lisaorban

There you can find all the latest news, blogs, interviews & free previews of all her books.

Printed in Poland
by Amazon Fulfillment
Poland Sp. z o.o., Wrocław